Old KINCARDINE

by
Marion Miller & Alex Shepherd

These Co-op buildings (photographed *c*.1925) were destroyed by a spectacular fire in 1930. The Co-op bakery, plus stabling for horses and accommodation for delivery vans, stood behind the building. The picture shows head butcher John Baikie and grocery manager Mr Maltman. The latter lived in a house to the left adjoining the shops.

First published in the United Kingdom, 1998
by Stenlake Publishing, Ochiltree Sawmill, The Lade,
Ochiltree, Ayrshire, KA18 2NX
Telephone / Fax: 01290 423114

ISBN 1 84033 020 1

ACKNOWLEDGEMENTS

With thanks to Heather Ross, Jenny MacCrimmon, Jean Thomson, James Park, Margaret Burt, Annie Wallace and Martin Millar for providing photographs and historical information. Many photographs came from the albums of the Shepherd family, with acknowledgement to the Ramsay and King families too.

The Mercat Cross pillar stands nearly nineteen feet high. It's not known precisely when it dates from, but it bears the coat of arms of the Earls of Kincardine (the Earldom was created in 1647). The cross was cut from blocks of stone from Longannet Quarry, which also provided the stone for the cross in Perth. A fair used to be held in the High Street on the second Friday in August, and included merry-go-rounds, stalls and donkey rides for the children. At night paraffin flares illuminated the sky.

INTRODUCTION

This house at 30 Kilbagie Street is typical of the architecture of old Kincardine. The outside stair gave access to a loft where fishing gear was stored and repaired during the winter months. Stowed masts protruded from the small bole window.

Kincardine, situated on the north bank of the River Forth, arose literally from the ashes. In the seventeenth to eighteenth centuries there were thirty-five local salt pans, evaporating sea water to produce salt, and large parts of the town are built on land reclaimed from the river using coal ash from these pans. Salt and coal were both exported by ship, forming the basis for a thriving ship-building industry.

There was a ferry in operation across the Forth from Kincardine as early as 1670. Cattle and horses were carried *en route* to the cattle market at Falkirk Tryst, with livestock driven down from Perth and given water in large stone troughs at the shore before making the crossing.

In 1843 the port of Kincardine was described as the most considerable on the Forth with the exception of Leith. Ships carrying local men sailed to destinations as far flung as the West Indies, Australia, the Mediterranean and the Baltic. By this time there were upwards of fifty ship-owners among Kincardine's population of 2,875. At the beginning of the nineteenth century there were often over a dozen ships under construction at any one time. These were destined for the Greenland fisheries, Baltic trade and East India trade. Ships queued up in the busy river, their hulls laden with cargo, and along with the ropeworks and sail-making industries the River Forth gave the people of Kincardine their livelihood.

The age of steam and larger ships saw the decline of shipbuilding and its related industries. Fishing, which also played an important part in Kincardine's past, didn't survive into the current century on any scale.

Once a part of Perthshire, the parishes of Kincardine and Tulliallan were transferred wholly to the County of Fife in 1891 by the boundary commissioners. In 1994 the people of Kincardine fought to remain in Fife when it was proposed that the town be incorporated into the new Clackmannan and Falkirk Council district. We are proud to be Fifers.

The coming of the bridge and the explosion of road transport saw the return of some prosperity to the town. Kincardine Power Station opened in the sixties, followed by Longannet. Today Kincardine is manned by a skeleton work-force, but Longannet Power Station employs many local people.

Sadly the once quiet town now has to suffer the effects of over 25,000 vehicles a day using the river crossing: a far cry from when its busiest time saw cattle being ferried from the north to the fairs at Falkirk. A long overdue new bridge is proposed for Kincardine, but as yet the Scottish Office hasn't decided where or when a new crossing will be built.

Marion Miller & Alex Shepherd

Chapel Square, now known as Elphinstone Street, in the early 1900s. The houses on both sides of the church were demolished to make way for the bridge road. The clock in the church tower was gifted by former local businessman Robert Maule in 1884. Coopers' Green, where fish barrels were stored, once occupied the site of the kirk. Kincardine public library now occupies the site of the ruined building on the right of this picture.

High Street, *c.*1904. The Commercial Hotel was built as the shipmaster's headquarters, and was the place where sailors gathered to pass on information about ships and recount their adventures at sea. Today it is Garvies lounge bar. A garvie was a small fish once caught on these shores in a wicker fish trap. Kincardine-born folk were known as garvies due to the quantity of the fish landed in the town. The small burn on the right, the overflow from an open mineral well, ran from Kirk Street.

Toll Road, Kincardine-on-Forth.

2201.

A 1920s photograph with the Tally Steven bus coming up Toll Road. The first house on the left, now the site of a day centre for the elderly, was home to Captain Rankine. Another sea-farer, Captain Alexander, lived across the road in the two storey house. The wall and trees (right, foreground) belonged to Roanhead Farm; the houses now occupying this stretch of road are called Roanhead Terrace. Toll Road is still the main road to Dunfermline.

Kincardine in more rural days, prior to the building of the bridge. The railway station and goods yard are visible (left), as is Stewart's Orchard (centre), and the haystacks at Burnbrae Steading (above the orchard).

This 1935 aerial view shows the start of big changes, with construction of the north bridge approach road under way (centre, foreground). The recently opened Fere Gait, with open fields to the right of it, is in the centre, with the lower part of Silver Street visible prior to demolition. The site of the kirk (top right) was once occupied by Tulliallan Distillery.

Remnants of The Bay during demolition as the route for the bridge approach road is prepared, 1935. After any saleable fixtures and fittings had been removed from the buildings, wire ropes were attached to them through doorways and windows, and the traction engine used to pull them down. This area of Kincardine had a long association with seafarers.

Chapel Square and The Bay during clearance work for the north bridge approach road. The size and style of the cement mixer is a bit different from today's models. Construction work was carried out by George Bald Contractors.

Prior to the building of the bridge the only means of crossing the Forth at Kincardine was by ferry. This picture, with the village of Airth in the background, shows the bridge under construction, with temporary gantries in place below it. The wires at the upper left were attached to the north pylon of Fife Electric's 132 kV cross-river supply lines.

The elegant structure of the 'Silver Link', as the bridge was known, showing wooden dolphins protecting the central piers. The movable swing span was the largest in the world, and turned 90° to provide two openings 150 feet wide for ships to pass through. Sadly with no more shipping it no longer needs to be used.

The interior of the bridge control room showing the main desk and relay control panels. The equipment was installed in 1936 and remains in place today, a tribute to its manufacturers and the operators who maintained it over fifty years of working life.

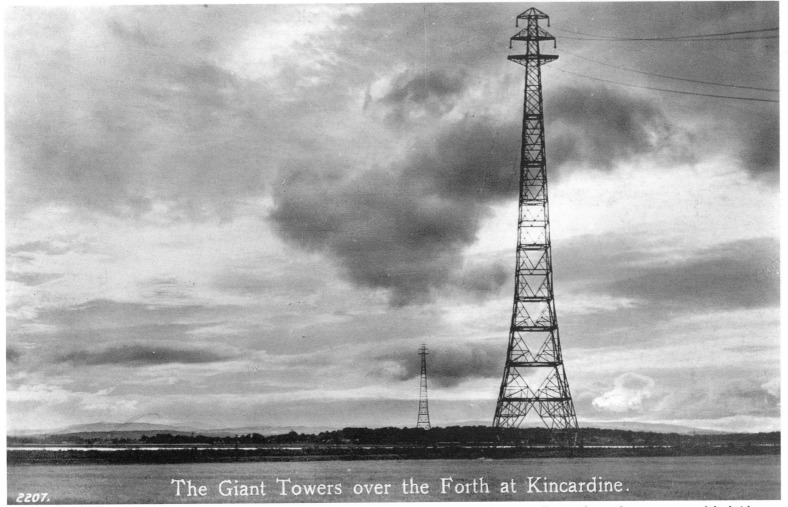

2207.

The Giant Towers over the Forth at Kincardine.

The Fife Electric Power Company's Forth Crossing towers have been removed and replaced by even taller 400 foot pylons upstream of the bridge.

Knowehead, Kincardine-on-Forth.

Knowehead Corner, at the west end of Elphinstone Street, 1917. The buildings on the left, once known as Salters Row, have all been demolished, and the council houses of Station Road now occupy their site. John Stock's bus, one of the first in the district, is parked next door to his wine and spirit shop. A baker's shop now stands on the site of the ruined building.

ELPHINSTONE STREET, KINCARDINE-ON-FORTH.

Mintoe's Close and J. Steel's Bakers and Grocers (with a car parked outside) have long since been demolished, as have the buildings of Knowehead Corner (background).

The Ferry or Low Pier with the Ochil Hills in the background. This pier (and its partner across the firth at Higginsneuk) was upgraded in 1826-1827.

THE PIER, KINCARDINE-ON-FORTH.

The Shipping or High Pier and the Kincardine to Dunfermline railway line. Grilse (young salmon) and mature salmon formed the bulk of the catch, and dealers bought the fish at so much per cran-load. At one time a rail spur ran out on to the pier, and having been packed into barrels the fish were loaded on to waggons for transportation. The spur was later lifted and a fish bank siding built near to Ferry Pier. There were many fishing smacks on the Forth and when the catch was good local boats were joined by vessels from Alloa, Bo'ness and Dunmore. Today there are only one or two small boats which catch the odd fish solely for pleasure.

The Promenade, Kincardine-on-Forth.

The promenade was once a favourite spot for walks but is now very overgrown. Fish bank siding can be seen to the left, with some fishing smacks on the river and salmon cobles moored at the shipping pier. Those on the pier are probably being repaired or recaulked. The timbers of an abandoned smack are visible above the water.

The Ferry Pier, 1928, with local salmon fishers showing off a good haul of 'the beastie'. The fish was weighed and packed in the hut to the right before being transported by rail to its destination. Most went to Billingsgate Market. The man on the far left is James Thomson, son of Bernard Thomson, who rented the fishing rights from the Crown Commissioners. B.T.K. stands for Bernard Thomson, Kincardine.

The Station, Kincardine.

The Alloa to Kincardine railway line opened on 18 December 1893, and the Dunfermline line was opened in 1906. At the turn of the century Kincardine Station was very busy in the summer months with holiday-makers coming to the seaside. Many travelled from Glasgow to this popular resort. Passenger traffic ceased during the early thirties, although goods traffic continued and increased during construction of the bridge and again with the building of the power stations. Sadly the station fell into disrepair and was burned down by vandals. Nothing remains of it, but recently the line has been cleared and a coal train now services the power stations.

GENERATING STATION, KINCARDINE ON FORTH. A3595

On the pier (left foreground) are James Thomson's buildings where salmon were landed, weighed and despatched by rail. The new sea wall is visible to the right, with the second phase of the power station under construction behind it.

George Meikle's well-known drapers shop in Elphinstone Street, decorated for the Coronation of Queen Elizabeth.

Keith Street was named after Admiral Lord Keith, who acquired Tulliallan Estate in 1798. Meikle's drapers was one of two shops Geordie Meikle had in the village. Geordie was famous for stocking everything under the sun, and if he didn't have something you wanted, he'd get it for you the next day!

Kincardine House

In 1902 Kincardine House was being used as 'Miss Nelson's Seminary for Young Ladies'. In later years it was leased to the Heggan family; Johnnie Heggan was well known in the community as a market gardener. The house has now been converted into flats called Orchard Grove. The dovecot, stables and barn have been demolished.

The class of 1933-34 photographed outside the new Tulliallan school in Kirk Street.

Back row: A. Forsyth; J. McLeod; G. Fleming; R. Drysdale; D. Scott; D. McMillan; R. Ross; C. Donaldson; B. Gray; J. Johnstone.

Third row: Miss H. Richardson (teacher); J. Gray; N. Chalmers; C. Kelly; S. Lawrence; M. Gilbert; P. Philip; M. McKenzie; E. King; unknown;
C. McIntyre; C. Miller.

Second row: H. Scotland; D. Moffat; C. Colligan; H. Davis; A. Young; H. Wilson; J. Birrell; E. Izatt; E. Leonard; J. Gillon; K. McGahie.

Front row: B. Campbell; W. Smart; S. Carr; R. Burns; J. McCluskey; A. Jenkins; J. Innes; W. McKenzie; A. Blair; J. Patterson; J. McAinsh; D. Walls.

Public School, Kincardine.

Children assemble in front of the 'new' public school which opened on 12 January 1889. It replaced the five private schools which had previously operated in Kincardine and Tulliallan parishes. Kincardine Subscription School previously stood on the site. The building glimpsed back right had been the headmaster's house and was later converted into a gymnasium. It is still in use today as part of the community centre.

Tulliallan School's first ever hockey team, started by Miss Pearl Russell, 1936. Well known faces include Agnes Wooler; Annie Millar; Effie Izatt; Jessie Denholm and Effie McAra.

KILBAGIE STREET, KINCARDINE.

The milk float just visible in the picture was owned by Kate Kinloch; the milk horse was called Donald. The white building at the far end of the street was part of a local brewery, and was known as the Barns. Its site is now occupied by the Masonic Lodge Hall. Apart from that, this part of Kilbagie Street remains much the same today as it was in the early 1900s.

No. 8 Kilbagie Street with the corner of John Steele's bakers to the right. This 1930s picture shows off the fine old marriage stone, dated 1716. When the photograph was taken this was one of the few really old buildings in Kincardine that was still lived in. The marriage stone was subsequently incorporated into council housing in Station Road.

Sands House. Kincardine-on-Forth

2006

Lord Sands' residence, just east of Kincardine, made an imposing sight until it was badly damaged by fire. Most of the ruins were subsequently demolished, although the small wing was later converted and used as a house. The grounds now contain a rose nursery.

32

Tulliallan Castle was built for retired admiral Lord Keith who acquired the Tulliallan Estate in 1798. The castle was built in an Italian design with landscaped gardens c.1820. After the estate was sold to the Scottish Office in 1954 the house became a police training college. Police men and women from all over Scotland are trained there, and the college also plays host to overseas forces. It employs many local people, and in 1996 new accommodation, a conference room, theatre, classrooms, a mock courtroom, shop, post office and bar were added to the complex.

Curlers at the opening of Tulliallan Curling Pond, adjacent to the Moor Loch. Sir James and Lady Sivewright, who provided the site and building, are prominent in the picture. The loch itself was previously used for curling, and when the ice was of the required thickness and a big match was on the school often closed so all could go and watch. Ice was cut from the loch and stored in an ice house on the Tulliallan Estate for keeping food fresh.

Tulliallan Bowling Club dates back to 1887 and the original pavilion was opened in May 1891. This picture shows the official opening of the reconstructed pavilion in May 1925. Rev. John McLaren, minister of Tulliallan parish church, officially opened the new pavilion and Mrs McLaren threw the first jack. The silver cup was provided by the local paper mill and was known as the Kilbagie Cup.

A victorious Tulliallan Thistle football team. During the twenties the team played at White Sink Park, which subsequently became part of the golf course.

The local cricket team also played at White Sink Park. Back row: J. Smith; G. Scotland; D. Pick; J. Maltman; T. Finlayson; J. Gordon; Mr Brown; J. Forsyth. Middle row: J. Stoddart; J. Boyd; P. Stoddart; R. Barnet; A. McLelland. Front row: S. Carr (scribe); D. Campbell.

Garage owner J. McHattie (owner of the car), accompanied by Tommy Millar, Jimmy Sorley and Bert King. All were keen golfers and helped with the setting up and running of the golf course.

Kilbagie Street and Chapelhill Street, Kincardine on Forth

The white building was Harry Kinloch's smiddy. The Manse Glebe can just be seen to the left.

James Dick, manager of Kincardine Gas Works, photographed with his wife and a worker. Before the advent of central heating a barrowload of hot cinders was wheeled along to Kincardine UP Church and take round the aisles to taken the chill off the building before a service.

Mr and Mrs J. Morgan show off their wares outside their house in Silver Street, 1910. The cycles were stored and repaired in a workshop at rear of house which was still in use until a few years ago.

The kirk in the background, Tulliallan's second, was built in 1675 and was in use until the present building opened in 1833. The kirkyard contains many interesting tombstones inscribed to ship-owners, ship-builders and merchant seamen. Details of their fates include drownings and shipwreckings off the coast of Africa. Meviston village, which once stood in the foreground, was cleared by Lord Keith, who also closed the old Perth Drove Road which ran beside churchyard wall as both were close to his new mansion house. The houses of Woodlea now occupy the site.

Tulliallan old cemetery, showing some of the interesting old tombstones decorated with tradesmen's symbols.

The Co-op drapery and dry goods department decorated with special window displays for George VI's Coronation celebrations. Manageress Miss McKenzie and assistant Miss E. King are in doorway. A glimpse of the now demolished Scotland's Close can be seen to the right through the railings.

The cottage adjoining the Auld Hoose is now a lounge bar connected to the pub. At one time the bar only consisted of a six-foot counter, and the seating comprised a bench on one wall. The Auld Hoose was well frequented when the shipyard across the road from it was in business. The marriage stone dated 1734 bears the initials of Ian Izat and Katherine Scotland.

Building work at Kincardine Power Station with overhead coal conveyors under construction.

The semi-circular building in the foreground was one of the workshops used during the building of the power station. A newly-built chimney is visible to the right.

The morning after torrential rain and flooding in Kilbagie Street, October 1954. Water levels had receded by about a foot by the time this picture was taken. There were further serious floods on 8 September 1979.

Wartime forces of law and order in Kincardine District, led by Sergeant A. Marnock and Corporal D. Bonthrone. The man at the centre of the back row is Dudley Watkins, creator of 'Oor Wullie'. He reputedly used Sergeant Marnock as the model for PC Murdoch in the comic strip!